A FOREVER FRIEND

Paintings by

Gay Talbott Boassy

HARVEST HOUSE PUBLISHERS

Eugene, Oregon 97402

A FOREVER FRIEND

©Gay Talbott Boassy

A teddy bear is a **FRIEND** like no other.

He is a constant companion and a loyal supporter.

He **LISTENS** with silent understanding,

keeps *every* secret, and

is always available for a great big hug.

He is **LOVING**, kind, honorable, brave,

polite, and devoted.

He is the good in all of us.

Best of all, a **TRUE BEAR**

never changes.

He is a **FOREVER** friend.

TOP SOIL

SEED

Peat Moss

FERTILIZER

© Gay Talbott Boassy

*F*or love is a flower that grows in any soil, works its sweet miracles undaunted by autumn frost or winter snow, blooming fair and fragrant all the year, and blessing those who give and those who receive.

LOUISA MAY ALCOTT
Little Men

To know someone here or there with whom you feel there is an understanding in spite of differences or thoughts unexpressed—that can make of this earth a garden.

GOETHE

Your Garden

First, plant six rows of "peas":

Praise, Patience, Preparedness,

Promptness, Perseverance, Politeness.

Then, plant five rows of "lettuce":

Let us be faithful.

Let us be loyal.

Let us be truthful.

Let us be unselfish.

Let us love one another.

AUTHOR UNKNOWN

*T*is friends who make this desert world
  To blossom as the rose—
Strew flowers o'er our rugged path,
Pour sunshine o'er our woes.

ANONYMOUS

Talbott-Boassy

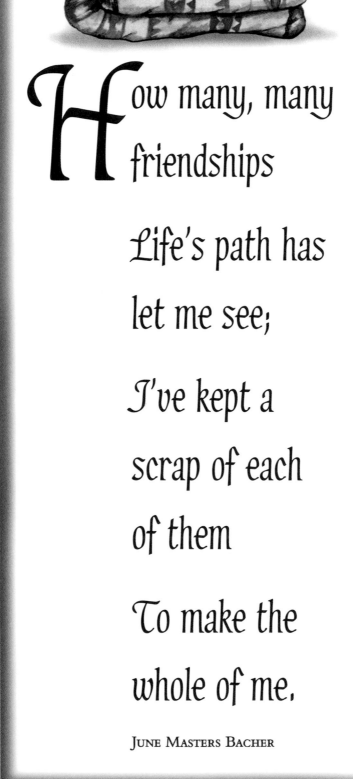

How many, many
friendships

Life's path has

let me see;

I've kept a

scrap of each

of them

To make the

whole of me.

JUNE MASTERS BACHER

© Gay Talbott-Boassy

9

It is one of the blessings of old friends that you can afford to be stupid with them.

A true friend is one who knows all about you and loves you just as you are,

Be completely humble

and gentle; be patient,

bearing with one

another in love.

THE BOOK OF EPHESIANS

With such a comrade, such a friend,
I fain would walk till journey's end,

Through summer sunshine, winter rain,

And then?—Farewell, we shall meet again!

HENRY VAN DYKE

Everyman,
I will go
with thee,
And be thy
guide,
In thy most
need to go
by thy
side.

ANONYMOUS

At every turning of the road
The strong arm of a comrade kind

To help me onward with my load...

FRANK DEMPSTER SHERMAN

© *Gay Talbott-Boassy*

FRIENDSHIP...serves a great host of different purposes all at the same time. In whatever direction you turn, it still remains yours. No barrier can shut it out. It can never be untimely; it can never be in the way. We need friendship all the time.

CICERO

© Gay Talbott Boassy

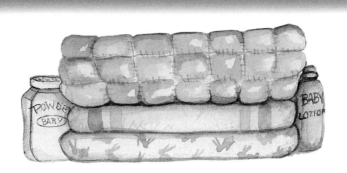

$\mathcal{E}$ach friend
represents a
world in us, a
world possibly
not born until
they arrive,
and it is only
by this meeting
that a new
world is born.

ANAIS NIN

He helped her in many ways, proving himself a true friend, and Jo was happy...

LOUISA MAY ALCOTT
Little Women

A good friend is like a wonderful book... The inside is even better than the cover!

ANONYMOUS

© Gay Talbott-Boassy

LITTLE BEARS

LITTLE MEN

LITTLE WOMEN

A friend is a volume of sympathy
bound in cloth.

AUTHOR UNKNOWN

© Gay Talbott-Boassy

*L*earn to put aside your own desires so that you will become patient.... This will make possible the next step, which is for you to enjoy other people and to like them, and finally you will grow to love them deeply.

THE BOOK OF 2 PETER

To have a
friend is one of
the sweetest
gifts that life
can bring.

AMY R. BROWN

A
friend is a gift you give yourself.

ROBERT LOUIS STEVENSON

© Gay Talbott-Boassy

Two are better than one, because they have a good return for their work.

© Gay Talbott-Boassy

If one falls down, his friend can help him up...

THE BOOK OF ECCLESIASTES

© Gay Talbott-Boassy

Friendship delights in the addition of the third or fourth party,

© Gay Talbott-Boassy

who, if they too are friends, only heighten the enjoyment of an occasion.

C.S. LEWIS

Practice tenderhearted mercy and kindness to others. Don't worry about making a good impression on them but be ready to suffer quietly and patiently. Be gentle and ready to forgive; never hold grudges...most of all, let love guide your life...

THE BOOK OF COLOSSIANS

No one is useless in this world
who lightens the burdens of it
for another.

CHARLES DICKENS

A good deed is never lost;
he who sows courtesy
reaps friendship, and
he who plants kindness
gathers love.

BASIL

Real friendliness is empathy
And being understood...
It's ceasing never, striving ever
For another's good.

ESTHER THOM

©Gay Talbott-Boassy

If you love someone you will be loyal to him no matter what the cost. You will always believe in him, always expect the best of him, and always stand your ground in defending him.

THE BOOK OF 1 CORINTHIANS

A loyal friend who never fails
To convey a thought of love,
Is in every way a blessing sent
From God in heaven above…

P.F. Freeman

Friendship improves happiness
and abates misery, by doubling
our joy and dividing our grief.

JOSEPH ADDISON

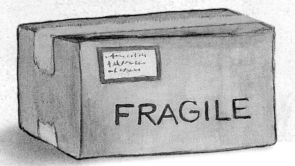

There is no friend
like an old friend
Who has shared
our morning days,
No greeting like
his welcome,
No homage like
his praise.

OLIVER WENDELL HOLMES

Friendship is one of the sweetest joys of life.

Charles H. Spurgeon

A true friend unbosoms freely, advises justly, assists readily, adventures boldly, takes all patiently, defends courageously, and continues friends unchangeably.

WILLIAM PENN

It doesn't take
an awful lot
To build a
world of love,
Some patience,
kindness,
and concern
With help from
God above.

OPAL McGUIRE DAVIS

Little kindnesses...
little appreciations,
little confidences...
they are all that are
needed to keep
the friendship sweet.

HUGH BLACK

Friendship…is born at the moment when
one man says to another "What! You too?
I thought that no one but myself…"

C.S. LEWIS

Friendship needs no studied phrases,
Polished face or winning wiles;
Friendship deals no lavish praises,
Friendship dons no surface smiles.

Friendship follows nature's diction,
Shuns the blandishments of art,
Boldly severs truth from fiction,
Speaks the language of the heart.

AUTHOR UNKNOWN

*T*here is nothing so precious as a faithful friend, and no scales can measure his excellence.

AUTHOR UNKNOWN

I'd like to be the sort of friend
that you have been to me.
I'd like to be the help that
you've been always glad to be.
I'd like to mean as much to
you each minute of the day
As you have meant, old
friend of mine, to
me along the
way.

EDGAR A. GUEST

Love bears all things, believes
all things, hopes all things,
endures all things.
Love never fails.

THE BOOK OF
1 CORINTHIANS

©Gay Talbott Boassy

I always felt that the great high privilege, relief and comfort of friendship was that one had to explain nothing.

KATHERINE MANSFIELD

True happiness consists not in

the multitude of friends, but in

their worth and choice.

BEN JOHNSON

Pooh, *promise* you won't

forget about me, ever. Not

even when I'm a hundred."

Pooh thought for a little.

"How old shall I be then?"

"Ninety-nine."

Pooh nodded.

"I promise," he said.

Still with his eyes

on the world Christopher

Robin put out a hand

and felt for Pooh's paw.

A.A. Milne
The House at Pooh Corner

There are no friends like old friends

And none so good and true;

We greet them when we meet them,

As roses greet the dew;

No other friends are dearer,

Though born of kindred mold;

And while we prize the new ones,

We treasure more the old.

There are no friends like old friends

Where'er we dwell or roam,

In lands beyond the ocean,

Or near the bounds of home;

And when they smile to gladden,

Or sometimes frown to guide,

We fondly wish those old friends

Were always by our side.

DAVID BANKS SICKLES

There is a fellowship
between
     A bond intangible,
     unseen,
     And yet so strong,
     its golden string
     Will bear the weight
     of anything
     And draw you closer
     year by year,
     And every day a bit
     more dear.

 EDNA JACQUES

O h, Bear!" said
Christopher Robin.
"How I do
love you!"
"So do I,"
said Pooh.

A.A. MILNE
Winnie-the-Pooh